PORTLAND
TRAIL BLAZERS

by Travis Clark

THIS BOOK CONTAINS AT LEAST 10% RECYCLED MATERIALS.

Editor: J Chris Roselius
Copy Editor: Anna Comstock
Series design: Christa Schneider
Cover production: Marie Tupy
Interior production: Carol Castro

Photo Credits: David Zalubowski/AP Images, cover; David Bergman/AP Images, 1; Dick Raphael/NBAE/Getty Images, 4, 21, 42 (top); JV/AP Images, 7; Rusty Kennedy/AP Images, 8, 15; Ed Kolenovsky/AP Images, 10; JES/AP Images, 13; Shane Young/AP Images, 16, 42 (middle), 47; Fred Jewell/AP Images, 18, 31, 42 (bottom), 43 (top); Lennox McLendon/AP Images, 23; Mark Elias/AP Images, 24; Scott Troyanos/AP Images, 26; John Swart/AP Images, 29, 44; Gary Stewart/AP Images, 32; Rick Bowmer/AP Images, 34; Ann Heisenfelt/AP Images, 37; Greg Wahl-Stephens/AP Images, 38, 43 (middle); Tony Gutierrez/AP Images, 41, 43 (bottom)

Library of Congress Cataloging-in-Publication Data
Clark, Travis, 1985-
  Portland Trail Blazers / by Travis Clark.
      p. cm. -- (Inside the NBA)
  ISBN 978-1-61783-173-7
  1. Portland Trail Blazers (Basketball team)--History--Juvenile literature. I. Title.
  GV885.52.P67C53 2012
  796.323'640979549--dc23
                                    2011021379

TABLE OF CONTENTS

Chapter 1 .... Unlikely Champions, 4

Chapter 2 .... Getting Started, 10

Chapter 3 .... A Decade of Success and Disappointment, 18

Chapter 4 .... Staying in Contention, 26

Chapter 5 .... Still Coming Up Short, 34

Timeline, 42

Quick Stats, 44

Quotes and Anecdotes, 45

Glossary, 46

For More Information, 47

Index, 48

About the Author, 48

UNLIKELY CHAMPIONS

T he city of Portland, Oregon, had caught "Blazermania" in 1977. The Portland Trail Blazers were contenders for their first National Basketball Association (NBA) title.

The Trail Blazers entered the NBA in 1970, but did not post a winning record until that 1976–77 season. The Trail Blazers finished the regular season 49–33 to clinch a playoff spot for the first time.

Two talented big men, 6-foot-11 center Bill Walton and 6-foot-9 forward Maurice Lucas, were the leaders of the team. During the regular season, Walton averaged 18.6 points and 14.4 rebounds per game. Lucas led Portland with 20.2 points per game and added 11.4 rebounds per game. And four other players, forward Bob Gross and guards Lionel Hollins, Dave Twardzik, and

Bill Walton (32) of the Portland Trail Blazers shoots against the Boston Celtics during an NBA game in the 1970s.

"Blazermania"

"We were down and out, and every-body was trash talking and telling us we were done, the series was over. But Jack Ramsay said, 'Guys, we are just getting started. We are not changing a thing. We just haven't played Blazers basketball yet.' We flew home, and there were 20,000 fans waiting at the Portland airport. They lined the highway, they laid flowers, brownies, and music on my front porch. The Blazermaniacs turned it around for us. We would have never achieved what we did without their undying love and their ability to inspire us and make us better than we were ever capable of by ourselves."
—Bill Walton on the importance of the fans' "Blazermania" during the 1977 NBA Finals

Larry Steele, all averaged more than 10 points per game.

The Trail Blazers defeated the Chicago Bulls two games to one in the first round of the Western Conference playoffs. Portland then eliminated the Denver Nuggets in six games in the second round. And they swept the Los Angeles Lakers in four games in the conference finals. The Trail Blazers were only four wins away from their first NBA title.

All the Trail Blazers had left to do was beat the powerful Philadelphia 76ers in the NBA Finals. The Sixers had finished the regular season with the best record in the Eastern Conference at 50–32. Leading Philadelphia was future Hall of Famer Julius "Dr. J" Erving. Behind Erving, the 76ers won the first two games of the best-of-seven series in Philadelphia, 107–101 and 107–89 respectively.

The series then headed to Portland. In Game 3, Walton had 20 points, 18 rebounds, and nine assists. Lucas added 27 points to lead Portland to a 129–107 victory. The Trail Blazers evened the series with a 130–98 win in Game 4.

Maurice Lucas of the Trail Blazers hauls down a rebound as Philadelphia's Darryl Dawkins battles for position during their NBA Finals game in 1977.

The two teams headed back to Philadelphia for Game 5. The Sixers had the better regular-season record, so they held home-court advantage in the series. If Portland was going to win the NBA title, it would need to win at least one game on the road.

First Home

Memorial Coliseum, the Portland Trail Blazers' original home, opened in 1960. Built to seat 12,000 people, the arena was usually sold out for every home game in the 25 years the Blazers used it. Today, the Coliseum is home to the Portland Winterhawks, a team in the Western Hockey League. The Trail Blazers now play in the Rose Garden.

The Portland Trail Blazers' Lionel Hollins continues to dribble as he slips in front of Philadelphia 76ers guard Henry Bibby in 1977.

Walton, Lucas, and Gross made sure they got the win in Game 5. Portland built a 91–69 lead with eight minutes remaining in the game. The 76ers rallied, but the Trail Blazers held on and claimed a 110–104 win. Gross scored 25 points that game to lead the Blazers, while Lucas had 20 points and 13 rebounds. Walton also contributed, scoring 24 points and grabbing 14 rebounds.

Portland headed home for Game 6 with a 3–2 series lead. Blazermania, as it was being called, was in full force among fans. Despite a 4:30 a.m. arrival time at the airport, more than 5,000 fans greeted the team. The city was ready to celebrate a championship. All the Trail

Blazers had to do was win one more game.

Walton was outstanding in Game 6. He scored 20 points, grabbed 23 rebounds, blocked eight shots, and handed out seven assists. The Blazers were clinging to a two-point lead with eight seconds remaining. Erving missed a jump shot that would have put Philadelphia ahead. His teammates, World B. Free and George McGinnis, each got off shots in the final seconds, but both were unsuccessful.

For the first time in team history, the Portland Trail Blazers were NBA champions. And the title came in only their seventh season as a team. Portland fans had every reason to believe a second one would come soon. However, through 2010–11, those fans were still waiting.

RIP CITY

To begin the 2009–10 season, the Portland Trail Blazers celebrated their fortieth anniversary in unique fashion. The starting lineup took the floor wearing their traditional home white jerseys. But instead of "Trail Blazers" on the front, the jerseys displayed the phrase "Rip City."

The nickname was created during the team's first season in 1970–71. On the night of February 18, 1971, Portland play-by-play announcer Bill Schonely used the phrase to describe a wild shot taken by guard Jim Barnett against the Los Angeles Lakers. Somehow, the shot went into the basket.

"Rip City! All night!" Schonely shouted. The phrase was used even more often during the 1976–77 season. Bill Walton and Maurice Lucas led a high-scoring Trail Blazers team that "ripped the nets" en route to the club's only NBA Championship.

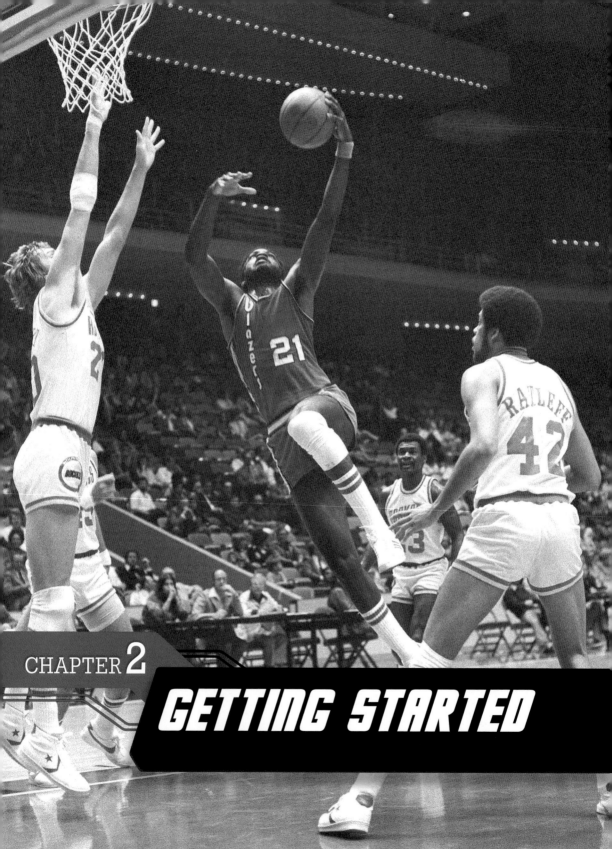

CHAPTER **2**

GETTING STARTED

T he NBA was growing rapidly near the end of the 1960s. The league had only nine teams in 1965. But by the 1969–70 season, 14 teams were in the league. And for the 1970–71 season, that number had grown to 17.

The Portland Trail Blazers were one of the three teams to enter the league that year. They were joined by the Cleveland Cavaliers and the Buffalo Braves.

The Trail Blazers hired Rolland Todd, the basketball coach at the University of Nevada, Las Vegas, to become the team's first head coach. Playing at home, Portland won its first game, beating Cleveland 115–112. Expansion teams often have trouble winning, however, and the Blazers were no exception. They finished the season just 29–53.

Guard Geoff Petrie had a good first year for Portland.

Sidney Wicks (21) of Portland jumps around Kevin Kunnert, *left*, and Ed Ratleff, *right*, of the Houston Rockets to score in 1976.

He averaged 24.8 points per game to lead the team. Guard Jim Barnett chipped in with 18.5 points per game in his only season in Portland. And center Leroy Ellis averaged 15.9 points and 12.3 rebounds per game.

Other than the veteran Ellis, the rest of the Blazers' roster was full of young players. During their first six seasons, Portland averaged only 28 wins and went through four different coaches. But the Blazers started to show improvement under coach Lenny Wilkens, who was hired in 1974.

Right away, Wilkens got some help. The Blazers selected center Bill Walton from the University of California, Los Angeles with the first pick in the 1974 NBA Draft. A star for UCLA, Walton, with help from fourth-year forward Sidney Wicks, helped the Trail Blazers go 38–44 in his first season.

In 1973–74, they won only 27 games. Walton averaged 12.8 points per game and a team-leading 12.6 rebounds per game. And Wicks led the Blazers with 21.7 points per game and averaged 10.7 rebounds per game.

Wilkens left Portland after the 1975–76 season, in which the Blazers went 37–45. He became coach of the Seattle Super-Sonics. Veteran coach Jack Ramsay was hired to replace him in Portland. Ramsay immediately made some changes to the roster. Wicks was sold to

Portland Trail Blazers guard Dave Twardzik, *right*, drives past Cleveland Cavaliers forward Campy Russell, *left*, for two points in 1979.

Boston. Ramsay also traded Petrie and Steve Hawes to Atlanta for the second pick in the American Basketball Association (ABA) dispersal draft.

The Blazers used that pick to take Maurice Lucas. He had played for the Kentucky Colonels in the ABA before the league merged with the NBA prior to the 1976–77 season. Lucas was known as a tough inside defender. He was a great addition and helped Walton on the defensive end of the court.

With Lucas and Walton, guards Dave Twardzik and Larry Steele, and forward Bob Gross, the Blazers won a team-record 49 games. They beat the Philadelphia 76ers in six games to win the NBA title in 1977.

But the team record for wins did not last long. The next

THE ENFORCER

A tremendous defensive player, Maurice Lucas played a big role in Portland's championship-winning season. The power forward was nicknamed "The Enforcer" and cleared the path for his frontcourt teammate Bill Walton. Lucas would only spend three and a half seasons in Portland. He later played for the New Jersey Nets, the New York Knicks, the Phoenix Suns, the Los Angeles Lakers, and the Seattle SuperSonics. He then returned for one last season in Portland in 1987–88. Lucas died in 2010 after a battle with cancer. After his death, former coach Jack Ramsay wrote about him on ESPN.com.

"Gone is The Intimidator of the 1976-77 championship Trail Blazers—the macho man with the bulging biceps and menacing stare. Luke was the physical spirit of that team. He enjoyed intimidating opponents and began each game by delivering a few sharp elbows to any who crossed his path."

season, 1977–78, Portland won 58 games—nine more than they had the previous year. Walton led the team in scoring and rebounding, averaging 18.9 points and 13.2 rebounds per game.

Lucas was second on the team in scoring and rebounding. He averaged 16.4 points and 9.1 rebounds per game. And third-year guard Lionel Hollins averaged 15.9 points and 4.7 assists per game.

Portland started that season winning 50 of its first 60 games. But injuries to Walton and Lucas hurt the team down the stretch. The Blazers went 8–14 in their final 22 games. Still, they won the Pacific Division title and got a bye in the first round of the playoffs.

Their hopes of repeating as NBA champions, however, ended in the Western Conference semifinals. Seattle and

Sidney Wicks (21) of the Portland Trail Blazers tries to dribble past Steve Mix of the Philadelphia 76ers during a 1976 game.

former coach Wilkens defeated Portland in six games. Walton suffered a fractured bone in his left foot in Game 2 and was forced to miss the rest of the series.

"I got a good lesson in humility when, in my second year in Portland, after a 50–10 start in the season, we had a rash of injuries to key players and won only eight of the remaining 22 games, and lost to Seattle in our first round of the playoffs," Ramsay wrote later in his life.

Despite missing 24 games, Walton was named the NBA's Most Valuable Player (MVP). Injuries had sidelined Walton during parts of his first three seasons in the league. And they would continue to haunt him for the rest of his career.

Coach Jack Ramsay during a special 25th anniversary reunion of the
Trail Blazers' 1976–77 championship team in 2002.

Walton played only 35 games his rookie season in 1974–75. He appeared in only 51 games the next season. In 1976–77, he played in only 65 games, and then in only 58 games his MVP season. That turned out to be his last season with Portland.

In 1978–79, Walton could not play due to the fractured bone in his foot. Without their big man in the middle, Portland's record slipped to 45–37. Center Tom Owens played well and Lucas was again solid. But the team was not the same without Walton.

Making matters worse, the former MVP was upset with the way he was treated by doctors and refused to play for Portland when it appeared he was getting healthy. He left as a free agent before the 1979–80 season started, signing with the San Diego Clippers. Thirty years later, Walton would apologize for his actions.

"I regret that I wasn't a better person, a better player. I regret that I got hurt. I regret the circumstances in which I left the Portland Trail Blazers family, and I just wish I could do a lot of things over, but I can't," Walton said in 2009.

Without Walton, Lucas took over as the top player, leading the team with 20.4 points per game and grabbing a team-high 10.4 rebounds per game. Owens, Hollins, and rookie Mychal Thompson also had good seasons. Portland finished 45–37, but lost to the Phoenix Suns in the first round of the playoffs.

The Blazers made several changes before and during the

Big Red

One of the key players on the 1977 championship-winning Trail Blazers was the center, Bill Walton. Known as the "Big Redhead," Walton suffered through repeated foot and knee injuries, keeping him from becoming an even better player than he was. Walton was enshrined into the Naismith Memorial Basketball Hall of Fame in 1993.

1979–80 season. Guard Jim Paxson was drafted in 1979. Rookie forward Calvin Natt was acquired from the New Jersey Nets for Lucas and two first-round draft picks. In the 25 games Natt played for Portland, he led the team in scoring with 20.4 points per game.

Portland finished the season 38–44, earning a playoff spot. But the Trail Blazers once again lost to rival Seattle, falling in the first round. Losing in the playoffs would become common for Portland in the 1980s.

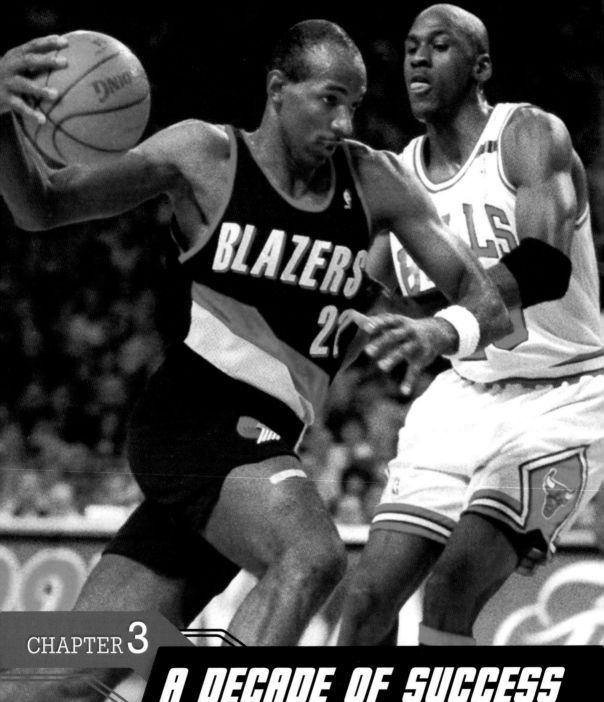

CHAPTER 3

A DECADE OF SUCCESS AND DISAPPOINTMENT

Bill Walton and Maurice Lucas were the foundation on which Portland's success was built in the 1970s. But as the 1980s began, the team had a new foundation. Shooting guard Jim Paxson and center Mychal Thompson became the top players for the Blazers in 1980–81.

Those two players were the heart of the new-look Trail Blazers, and the team posted a 45–37 record. Paxson averaged 17.1 points per game to lead the team. Thompson followed close behind, scoring 17 points per game. He was also second on the team in rebounding, averaging 8.7 per game. But for the third straight year, the Blazers lost in the first round of the playoffs. In a three-game series, the Kansas City Kings eliminated Portland two games to one.

That 1980–81 season summed up how the entire

The Portland Trail Blazers' Clyde Drexler, *left*, drives against the Chicago Bulls' Michael Jordan during Game 2 of the 1992 NBA finals.

decade would unfold. Portland maintained a hardworking, talented team that played with everything it had. However, playoff success would remain hard to grasp despite the improved play of Paxson and Thompson.

The two players carried the team in the early 80s, and they took turns as Portland's scoring leaders from 1981–1984. A strong supporting cast included Calvin Natt and Kenny Carr.

The Blazers missed the playoffs in 1982, despite having a 42–40 record. But they returned to the postseason in 1983 after finishing 46–36. That postseason berth would start a streak of 21 consecutive trips to the playoffs. Portland eliminated Seattle in the first round but lost to the Los Angeles Lakers in the conference semifinals.

In 1983, one of Portland's greatest players would join the team. The Trail Blazers drafted guard Clyde "The Glide" Drexler. He was an athletic and exciting talent from the University of Houston. He was known for his powerful slam dunks and quickness. But he still needed to refine his game for the NBA, so he started only three games in his rookie season.

The Blazers had another solid season in 1983–84, finishing 48–34. But then came

Kenny Carr (34) of the Portland Trail Blazers drives to the basket against Cedric Maxwell, *left*, of the Boston Celtics in 1984.

another short playoff appearance. This time, the Phoenix Suns defeated Portland in the first-round series in five games.

Despite the Trail Blazers' struggles in the postseason, the fans in Portland remained faithful to their team. Each home game was sold out and featured loud crowds. On March 3, 1984, the Coliseum hosted its 300th straight sold-out game.

In an effort to improve their postseason performances, the Trail Blazers made some moves during the 1984 offseason. Natt, center Wayne Cooper, guard Fat Lever, and two draft

CLYDE "THE GLIDE" DREXLER

One of the greatest players to ever wear a Portland uniform was Clyde "The Glide" Drexler. As of 2011, he is the all-time franchise leader in points scored, rebounds, and steals. And he is second all-time in assists.

"After Michael (Jordan), the gulf of talent between Clyde and everyone else in the league was so great," said former Portland star Geoff Petrie, the team's general manager from 1990-1994. "He was so much better. Just so quick, so fast, and so powerful. And people never realized what a great passer he was. Just a phenomenal athlete."

Drexler did not finish his career in Portland. In 1995, Drexler requested to be traded to a championship contender. The Blazers sent their star to the Houston Rockets. Drexler helped Houston win its second consecutive NBA title.

picks were traded to the Denver Nuggets for forward Kiki Vandeweghe. In addition, Portland selected center Sam Bowie—passing on future Hall of Fame guard Michael Jordan—and forwards Bernard Thompson and Jerome Kersey in the NBA Draft.

Vandeweghe contributed immediately to Portland. He led the Blazers in scoring with 22.4 points per game. Mychal Thompson scored 18.4 points per game, and Paxson added 17.9 points per game. And Drexler had a breakout season.

The second-year player increased his scoring average to 17.2 points per game and started 43 of the team's 82 games. Bowie also had a good season. He averaged 10 points and a team-leading 8.6 rebounds per game.

As a team, however, Portland struggled to win. The

Kiki Vandeweghe (55) of the Portland Trail Blazers shoots while the Lakers' James Worthy and Kareem Abdul-Jabbar attempt a block in 1985.

Blazers finished with a 42–40 record. They defeated the Dallas Mavericks three games to one in the first round of the playoffs. But the Lakers eliminated them in the Western Conference semifinals in five games.

In the 1985 NBA Draft, the Blazers added another key player. They picked guard Terry Porter with the 24th overall selection. Fans had high hopes entering the 1985–86 season. Drexler was becoming a star. Paxson, Thompson, and Vandeweghe were experienced players. Porter would add another young player off the bench. It looked like Ramsay

Trail Blazers forward Jerome Kersey and Chicago Bulls forward Scottie Pippen battle for control of the ball during a 1989 game.

might be able to recreate the magic of 1977.

However, nothing seemed to go right for the Blazers that year. They fell to 40–42 and lost in the first round of the playoffs to Denver. Ramsay was fired after the season and replaced by Mike Schuler in 1986.

Under the leadership of Schuler, Drexler continued to improve. Vandeweghe was the leading scorer for the third straight year, averaging 26.9 points per game. But Drexler was quickly becoming the focal point of the team.

He averaged 21.7 points per game in 1986–87. Porter improved as well. Starting 80 games for Portland, he scored 13.1 points per game and led the team in assists with 8.9 per game. Rookie center Kevin Duckworth also had a strong first season.

The Blazers were an improved team in the win column as well. They finished 49–33. Schuler earned Coach of the Year honors. Nevertheless, the Houston Rockets beat Portland in the first round of the playoffs. It was the third time in four years the Blazers had failed to advance past the first round.

Portland was even better in Schuler's second season, 1987–88. Drexler had his best season yet. He scored a career-high 27 points per game. Forward Jerome Kersey had his best season as well, averaging 19.2 points and a team-best 8.3 rebounds per game.

The Blazers finished the season 53–29, their highest

Michael Who?

Portland has had several draft picks become stars during the team's history. Sam Bowie is not one of them. The Blazers took the center with the second overall pick in the 1984 NBA Draft. That allowed the Chicago Bulls to take guard Michael Jordan with the third pick. Bowie's career was slowed by a series of injuries. Jordan, on the other hand, went on to become a Hall of Fame player and winner of six NBA titles with the Bulls.

win total since 1977–78. But just as in the previous two seasons, they lost in the first round of the playoffs. The Utah Jazz eliminated them in four games.

Year after year, the Trail Blazers were successful during the regular season. But the team always fell short in the playoffs. Fans began to wonder if the Trail Blazers would ever find success.

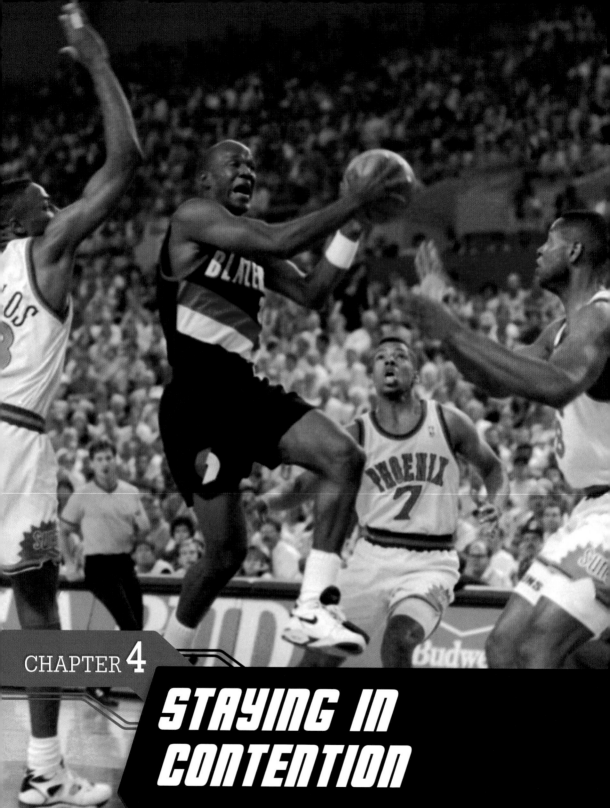

CHAPTER 4

STAYING IN CONTENTION

As the 1980s came to a close, Portland fans expected one last hurrah. Clyde Drexler was looking more and more like the Hall of Famer he would become. Terry Porter was an excellent point guard. And Kevin Duckworth and Jerome Kersey provided a strong presence in the middle.

One year after guiding the Blazers to a 53–29 record, a mediocre start to the season cost coach Mike Schuler his job. He was fired after going 25–22 after 47 games. Assistant coach Rick Adelman, a member of the first Portland team, was named the new coach. However, Adelman did not turn things around immediately.

Portland finished the 1988–89 season with a 39–43 record, but still made the playoffs. For the fourth straight year, however, they lost in the

Portland's Terry Porter flies through the air between Phoenix Suns defenders to score early in a 1992 NBA playoff game.

first round. Adelman went just 14–21 after taking over as coach in 1989. But his time with the team proved to be valuable the following season.

Under his leadership in 1989–90, Portland would enjoy their best season since winning the title. Drexler, Porter, Duckworth, and Kersey lifted the Blazers to their first NBA Finals appearance since 1977.

As a team, Portland averaged more than 114.2 points per game to rank fourth in the NBA. After posting a 59–23 record during the regular season, the Blazers took on the Dallas Mavericks in the first round of the playoffs. For the first time since 1985, they advanced to the conference semifinals, sweeping the Mavericks in three games.

Portland then defeated the San Antonio Spurs in seven games to advance to

Coming Full Circle

Rick Adelman was a player on the Trail Blazers' original team in 1970. After his playing career ended, he joined the team as an assistant coach in 1983 under head coach Jack Ramsay. After new head coach Mike Schuler was fired in the 1988–89 season, Adelman was hired to fill his shoes. It was his first head-coaching job. He guided Portland to the NBA Finals in 1990 and 1992.

the conference finals for the first time since 1977. There, the Blazers faced the Phoenix Suns. In a high-scoring series, Portland won all three of its home games to win the series four games to two.

The win set up a showdown against the Detroit Pistons in the NBA Finals. The Pistons had won the title the previous year. And they were a tough, veteran team led by guards Isiah Thomas, Joe Dumars, and Vinnie Johnson. The magic of "Blazermania" did not lead

As of 2011, Portland Trail Blazers guard Clyde Drexler is the team's all-time leader in points scored, steals, total rebounds, and offensive rebounds.

to the repeated success of 1977. The Pistons won the series and championship in five games.

The Trail Blazers did not let the loss to Detroit carry into the 1990–91 season, though. Key players such as Drexler, Porter, Kersey, and Duckworth returned. And forward Cliff Robinson, who had joined Portland in 1989, was a fantastic player off the bench. The Blazers went 63–19, which was the best record in the NBA and the most wins in club history.

But despite their regular-season success, Portland was not able to return to the NBA Finals. The Blazers suffered disappointment in the conference

OVERSHADOWED, BUT NOT FORGOTTEN

During his career, Terry Porter developed into one of the NBA's best three-point shooters of all time. He made 773 three-pointers. As of 2011, that stood as the team record. Only Drexler, with 18,040 points, scored more points as a Trail Blazer. In his 10 seasons with Portland, Porter scored a total of 11,330 points. Porter's 5,319 assists is also a franchise record.

At the end of the 1994–95 season, Porter left Portland and headed to Minnesota to play for the Timberwolves. He played for two other teams in the next seven years. Porter retired in 2002 after 17 seasons in the NBA.

finals. The Los Angeles Lakers defeated Portland in six games.

Drexler was now at the top of his game. The shooting guard was named to the All-NBA Second Team at the end of the 1990–91 season. He led the team in points scored, and he averaged more than six rebounds and six assists per game. With Drexler playing so well, fans believed a championship was within reach.

After losing in the conference finals in 1991, the Blazers returned to the NBA Finals in 1992. They finished the season 57–25 and cruised through their opponents in the playoffs. They eliminated the Lakers, the Suns, and the Utah Jazz. In those three series, Portland lost only four games.

The Blazers then faced Michael Jordan and the

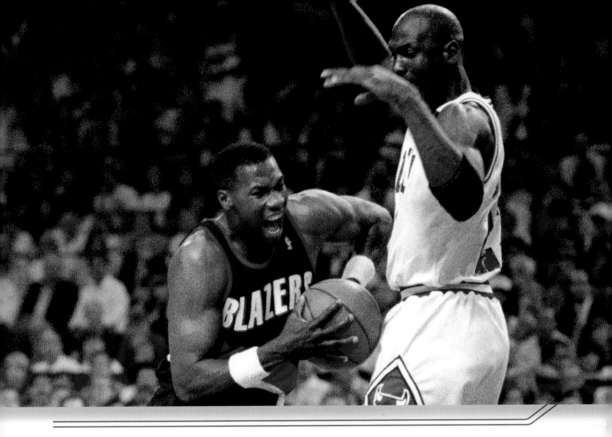

Portland forward Jerome Kersey, *left*, tries to get around Chicago Bulls guard Michael Jordan during Game 6 of the 1992 NBA Finals.

Chicago Bulls in the NBA Finals. Drexler against Jordan was a matchup of superstars. But the defending champion Bulls won the series in six games. The Bulls would win six titles in the 1990s.

From 1989 to 1992, the Blazers were one of the best teams in the NBA. They won 73 percent of their regular-season games during that time. However, that success did not carry over into the postseason. All it produced were two losses in the NBA Finals and one loss in the Western Conference finals.

Portland struggled even more in the postseason over the next few years. They lost in the first round of the playoffs in 1993 and 1994. Adelman was

Kevin Duckworth, *right*, and Clyde Drexler, *center*, try to block the shot of Seattle SuperSonics forward Shawn Kemp during a 1991 playoff game.

One Long Wait

In the 1986 NBA Draft, Portland selected center Arvydas Sabonis of Lithuania in the first round of the draft. Due to the political climate at that time, the Soviet Union, which Lithuania was a part of, would not allow him to play in the United States. It would not be until 1995 that he would finally put on a Blazers uniform.

fired after the 1993–94 season. P. J. Carlesimo was hired from Seton Hall University to replace Adelman.

Players were coming and going as well. Rod Strickland, who had joined the team in 1992, would replace Porter in the starting lineup. In addition, Robinson would take over for

Drexler midway through the 1994–95 season. On February 14, Drexler was traded to the Houston Rockets. He joined former University of Houston teammate Hakeem Olajuwon to lead the Rockets to the NBA title that season.

Drexler was gone, and Porter left for the Minnesota Timberwolves in 1995. Robinson and Strickland were next to go. Strickland and forward Harvey Grant were traded to the Washington Wizards for forward/center Rasheed Wallace

and guard Mitchell Butler. Robinson signed with Phoenix as a free agent in 1997.

Despite the change in the roster and a new head coach, the results would be the same as previous seasons. Portland played well during the regular season but fell short when it came to the playoffs.

The Blazers failed to advance past the first round of the playoffs during each of Carlesimo's three years as coach. Mike Dunleavy became the new head coach in 1997–98. But like Carlesimo, he failed to lead Portland past the first round of the playoffs.

Drexler and Porter were unable to win a title in Portland. Neither could Strickland and Robinson. Now it was up to Wallace to bring a championship to the city.

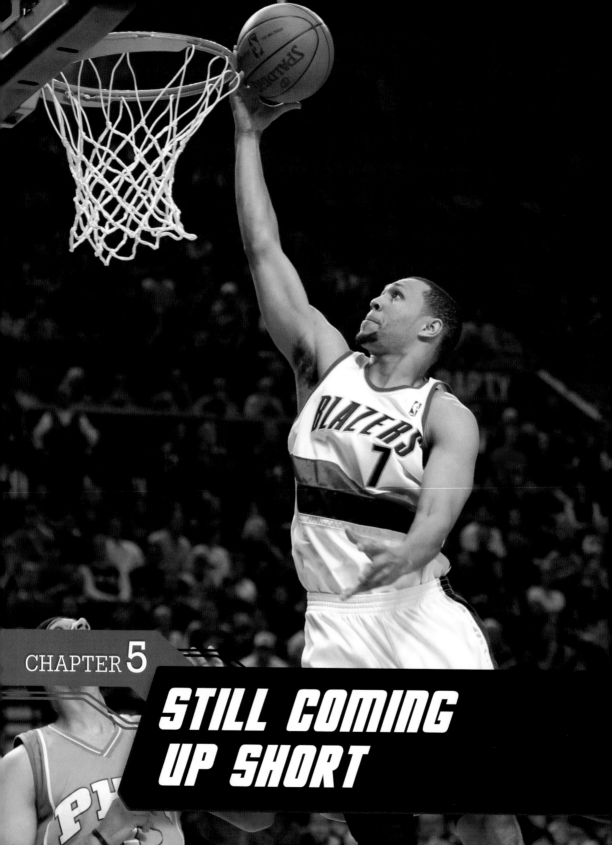

CHAPTER 5

STILL COMING UP SHORT

Under coach Mike Dunleavy, forward Rasheed Wallace became the new star in Portland. He was joined by a strong cast of players.

One of those players was Scottie Pippen, a key member of the Chicago Bulls during their championship years in the 1990s. Guards Greg Anthony, Damon Stoudamire, Isaiah Rider, Bonzi Wells, and Steve Smith gave the Blazers a deep backcourt. And forward Brian Grant and center Arvydas Sabonis gave Portland a strong frontcourt.

In the strike-shortened 1998–99 regular season, Portland finished 35–15. Rider led the team in scoring with 13.9 points per game.

In the first round of the 1999 postseason, the Blazers swept the Phoenix Suns in three games. In the conference semifinals, they eliminated the Utah Jazz in six games. But they were no match for the San

Portland guard Brandon Roy goes to the basket during Game 4 of an NBA first-round playoff series against the Phoenix Suns in 2010.

Adding a Hall of Famer

In 11 seasons with the Chicago Bulls, Scottie Pippen played an important supporting role to Michael Jordan. He helped the team win six championships in the 1990s. After one season in Houston, Pippen joined Portland in 1999–2000 and stayed for four seasons. He averaged just over 11 points per game during that time.

Antonio Spurs in the Western Conference finals. They swept Portland in four games.

In 1999–2000, Portland finished 59–23 and again earned a playoff spot. The Trail Blazers eliminated the Minnesota Timberwolves in the first round in four games. They faced Utah in a second-round rematch from the previous year. This time, Portland needed only five games to eliminate the Jazz. But as in 1999, the Blazers fell short of reaching the NBA Finals. The Los Angeles Lakers eliminated

them in seven games in the conference finals.

Portland finished 50–32 in 2000–01. When the Blazers lost in the first round of the playoffs in 2001, Dunleavy was fired. Portland hired Maurice Cheeks, an assistant coach with no head-coaching experience, to try to get the team over the hump.

In Cheeks's first two seasons, the Trail Blazers did well. They won 49 games in 2001–02, and 50 games in 2002–03. Wallace averaged almost 20 points per game both years. Like so many before him, however, Cheeks could not lead his team to victory in the playoffs. Both seasons ended in first-round defeats.

Back in 2001, Portland had drafted Zach Randolph. He was a power forward with good size and a left-handed shot. He came off the bench most of the time

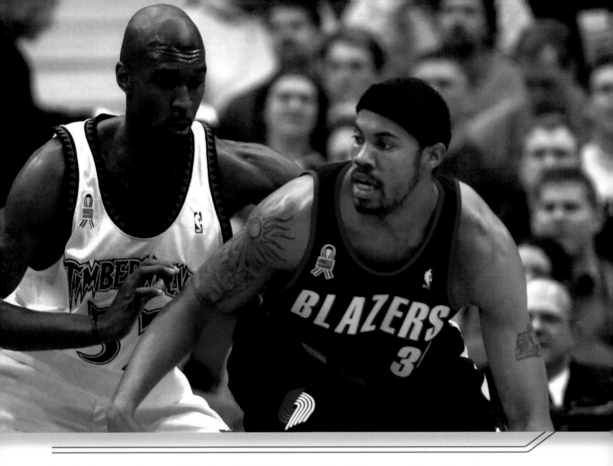

Trail Blazers forward Rasheed Wallace, *right*, drives against Minnesota Timberwolves forward Joe Smith in 2002.

during his first two seasons. But in 2003–04, he became a top player after the Blazers traded Wallace to the Atlanta Hawks midway through the season.

Randolph led the team in scoring and rebounding with 20.1 points per game and 10.5 rebounds per game during the 2003–04 season. But as a team, the Trail Blazers could only manage a 41–41 record. For the first time in 22 years, they missed the playoffs completely. It would be the first in a string of five straight seasons without a playoff berth.

Portland fired Cheeks in 2005 after starting the season 22–33. Kevin Pritchard

Zach Randolph, *left*, of Portland works against the Toronto Raptors' Matt Bonner, *right*, during a game in 2004.

replaced him, but the move did not help. Portland finished just 5–22 under Pritchard, and ended the season with a 27–55 record.

Portland hired coach Nate McMillan during the offseason. The Blazers finished 21–61 in McMillan's first season in 2005–06. That was their worst record since finishing 21–61 in 1972–73.

But help was on the way. The Trail Blazers traded for two players during the 2006 NBA Draft who would become the new cornerstones of the team. The first trade sent Viktor Khryapa and Tyrus Thomas to the Chicago Bulls for power forward LaMarcus Aldridge and a 2007 second-round draft pick. The Blazers then traded Randy Foye to the Minnesota Timberwolves for guard Brandon Roy.

Aldridge and Roy did not turn the Blazers into immediate winners as Portland finished 32–50. But Roy averaged 16.8 points and four assists per game his first season. And he was named the 2006–07 NBA Rookie of the Year.

During the offseason, the Blazers created a spot in the starting lineup for Aldridge by trading Randolph to the New York Knicks. Roy and Aldridge were the new leaders of the team.

The remade Trail Blazers continued to improve. They finished an even 41–41 in 2007–08. And in 2008–09, they finished with a 54–28

A FUTURE STAR

Those who watched Brandon Roy play basketball as a youth saw a future star. A native of Seattle, Roy attended the University of Washington. There, he finished as the school's 10th all-time leading scorer with 1,477 points. Roy was named the Pac-10 Player of the Year, and he earned First Team All-America honors as a senior in 2005–06.

Roy was drafted by the Minnesota Timberwolves with the sixth overall pick in the 2006 NBA Draft. The Wolves immediately traded his rights to Portland for guard Randy Foye. Roy missed 25 games his rookie season due to injuries. But he was still named the NBA Rookie of the Year after averaging more than 16 points per game.

In 2009, Roy was the winner of the Magic Johnson Award, presented to an NBA player who combines excellence on the court with outstanding cooperation with the media.

record. It was their best win total since 1999–2000. The Blazers returned to the playoffs, but it was another first-round exit.

Portland finished 50–32 in 2009–10. Roy led the team with 21.5 points per game, and Aldridge added 17.9 points and eight rebounds per game. But for the second straight year, the Blazers were eliminated in the first round of the playoffs.

The team entered the 2010–11 season with high hopes. But Roy had to have knee surgery during the season and played in only 47 games, starting 23 of them.

Aldridge stepped up for Portland. He set career highs in scoring with 21.8 points per game and in rebounds with 8.8 per game. And second-year guard Wesley Matthews did a good job of filling in for Roy. He was second on the team in scoring with 15.9 points per game. In addition, veteran Andre Miller added 12.7 points and seven assists per game.

Those three players and the return of Roy helped the Blazers finish the regular season with a 48–34 record. They earned a spot in the play-offs as the sixth seed. The team took on the Dallas Mavericks in the first round and quickly fell behind in the series 2–0, losing both games in Dallas.

The series then headed west to Portland. The Blazers won Game 3 97–92. Portland

Portland Trail Blazers forward LaMarcus Aldridge, *left*, battles Dallas Mavericks center Tyson Chandler, *right*, during a 2011 NBA playoff game.

staged an amazing comeback in Game 4. Trailing 67–44 in the third quarter, the Blazers stormed back to win 84–82. Roy hit the game-winner when he sank a bank shot with 39.2 seconds remaining in the game. Roy scored 18 points in the fourth quarter and 24 points overall. He was mobbed by his teammates after the game.

Portland was unable to carry the momentum they gained in Game 4 into the rest of the series, though. The Mavericks eliminated them in six games. But fans in Portland have hope that their roster of young stars will soon return the Blazers to the NBA Finals.

TIMELINE

1970 — The Portland Trail Blazers play their first-ever game against the Cleveland Cavaliers on October 16. The Blazers win 115–112.

1974 — Portland drafts center Bill Walton of the University of California, Los Angeles with the first pick of the NBA Draft on May 28.

1976 — On August 5, forward Maurice Lucas joins Portland in the ABA Dispersal Draft. Jack Ramsay is named head coach.

1977 — Following their first winning season in team history, the Trail Blazers defeat the Philadelphia 76ers in six games to win the team's first NBA championship—their only one through 2010–11.

1983 — On June 28, future Hall of Famer Clyde Drexler of the University of Houston is chosen 14th overall in the NBA Draft by Portland.

1984 — During the NBA Draft, the Trail Blazers infamously pass on selecting Michael Jordan second overall, instead going with center Sam Bowie. Jordan went on to become a Hall of Famer, while Bowie suffered injuries throughout his career.

1988 — Jim Paxson becomes the first Portland player to reach 10,000 career points.

1990 — Portland reaches the NBA Finals for the first time in 13 years, but loses to the Detroit Pistons in five games.

1992	For the second time in three years, the Trail Blazers lose in the NBA Finals, coming up short against the Chicago Bulls.
1995	Clyde Drexler is traded to the Houston Rockets mid-season, ending his career with the Trail Blazers.
1995	The Blazers' new arena, named the Rose Garden, opens on October 12. Arvydas Sabonis makes his debut as a 31-year-old rookie in the 1995-96 season.
2000	For the second straight season, the Trail Blazers lose in the Western Conference Finals under coach Mike Dunleavy.
2004	With a record of 41-41, Portland misses out on the playoffs for the first time since the 1981–82 season.
2005	Coach Nate McMillan is hired from the Seattle SuperSonics after Portland lets go of interim coach Kevin Pritchard.
2007	With the first overall pick in the NBA Draft, the Portland Trail Blazers select center Greg Oden from Ohio State. Injuries mar the early stages of his NBA career, similar to Sam Bowie.
2009	The Trail Blazers make the playoffs for the first time after missing out five straight years.
2011	Portland advances to the Western Conference playoffs for the third year in a row after posting a 48–34 record. The Trail Blazers lose to the Dallas Mavericks in six games in the opening round.

QUICK STATS

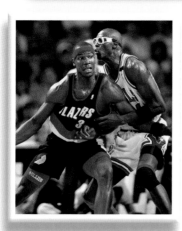

FRANCHISE HISTORY

Portland Trail Blazers (1970–)

NBA FINALS
(win in bold)

1977, 1990, 1992

CONFERENCE FINALS

1977, 1990, 1991, 1992, 1999, 2000

DIVISION TITLES

1978, 1991, 1992, 1999

KEY PLAYERS
(position[s]; years with team)

LaMarcus Aldridge (F; 2006–)
Clyde Drexler (G; 1983–95)
Kevin Duckworth (C; 1986–93)
Bob Gross (F; 1975–82)
Maurice Lucas (F; 1976–80)
Terry Porter (G; 1985–95)
Zach Randolph (F; 2001–07)
Cliff Robinson (F; 1989–97)
Brandon Roy (G; 2006–)
Arvydas Sabonis (C; 1995–2001, 2002–03)
Larry Steele (F; 1971–80)
Mychal Thompson (C/F; 1978–79, 1980–86)
Bonzi Wells (G; 1999–2003)
Sidney Wicks (C; 1971–76)

KEY COACHES

Rick Adelman (1989–94):
    291–154; 36–33 (postseason)
Nate McMillan (2005–):
    246–246; 6–12 (postseason)
Jack Ramsay (1976–86):
    453–367; 29–30 (postseason)

HOME ARENAS

Memorial Coliseum (1970–95)
Rose Garden Arena (1995–)

*All statistics through 2010–11 season

"I had one dream, and that was to be part of a special team and have a chance to be out there when the game was on the line." —Bill Walton on the 1977 championship-winning team

"Clyde plays with as much fire and determination as any player in the league. Just because he's laid-back off the court or doesn't seek recognition or hasn't been one of the superstars the league has chosen to market, doesn't change that. He's one of the fiercest competitors I've ever known." —Rick Adelman

After being awarded an expansion team in 1970, the Portland basketball team held a contest to name the team. The winner was "Pioneers," but that name was already being used by Lewis and Clark College in Portland. Trail Blazers received the second most votes and was selected as the team's nickname.

Bill Walton suffered through a severe stuttering problem until he was 28 years old. That is when he met Hall of Fame broadcaster Marty Glickman. During a brief conversation, Glickman told Walton that talking was a skill that needed to be developed. He gave Walton some tips to help him overcome his problem. And Walton did. He became a broadcaster himself after his playing career.

"I was an adrenaline player, I could definitely get psyched up for games. And I could take an ill-advised shot. That's the way I always played. But usually, it would go in. That's kind of the way I live my life: very spontaneous."—Jim Barnett, one of Portland's first players, talking about his playing career

GLOSSARY

assist

A pass that leads directly to a made basket.

backcourt

The point guards and shooting guards on a basketball team.

berth

A place, spot, or position, such as in the NBA playoffs.

contender

A team that is in the race for a championship or playoff berth.

decade

A period of 10 years.

draft

A system used by professional sports leagues to select new players in order to spread incoming talent among all teams. The NBA Draft is held each June.

expansion

In sports, the addition of a franchise or franchises to a league.

franchise

An entire sports organization, including the players, coaches, and staff.

free agent

A player whose contract has expired and who is able to sign with a team of his choice.

general manager

The executive who is in charge of the team's overall operation. He or she hires and fires coaches, drafts players, and signs free agents.

merge

Combine together.

postseason

The games in which the best teams play after the regular-season schedule has been completed.

rebound

To secure the basketball after a missed shot.

Further Reading

Ballard, Chris. *The Art of a Beautiful Game: The Thinking Fan's Tour of the NBA*. New York: Simon & Schuster, 2009.

Halberstam, David. *The Breaks of the Game*. New York: Knopf, 1981.

Thompson, Wayne. *Blazermania: This is Our Story—The Official History of Portland Trail Blazers*. San Rafael, CA: Insight Editions, 2010.

Web Links

To learn more about the Portland Trail Blazers, visit ABDO Publishing Company online at **www.abdopublishing.com**. Web sites about the Trail Blazers are featured on our Book Links page. These links are routinely monitored and updated to provide the most current information available.

Places to Visit

Memorial Coliseum
300 North Winning Way
Portland, OR 97208
503-797-9619
www.rosequarter.com
Original home arena of the Trail Blazers, the Memorial Coliseum now plays host to a minor league hockey team.

Naismith Memorial Basketball Hall of Fame
1000 West Columbus Avenue
Springfield, MA 01105
413-781-6500
www.hoophall.com
This hall of fame and museum highlights the greatest players and moments in the history of basketball. Former Trail Blazers Jack Ramsay, Bill Walton, and Clyde Drexler are enshrined here.

Rose Garden
One Center Court, Suite 150
Portland, OR 97227
503-963-4400
www.rosequarter.com
The home arena for Portland since 1995, the Trail Blazers play 41 home games a year here. Located in the city's Rose Quarter, tours are available when the team is not in town.

INDEX

Adelman, Rick (player and coach), 27–28, 31–32
Aldridge, LaMarcus, 39–40
Allen, Paul (owner), 33
Anthony, Greg, 35

Barnett, Jim, 9, 12
Bowie, Sam, 22, 25
Butler, Mitchell, 33

Carlesimo, P. J. (coach), 32–33
Carr, Kenny, 20
Cheeks, Maurice (coach), 36–37
Cooper, Wayne, 21

Drexler, Clyde, 20, 22–25, 27–31, 33
Duckworth, Kevin, 25, 27–29
Dunleavy, Mike (coach), 33, 35–36

Ellis, Leroy, 12

Foye, Randy, 39

Grant, Brian, 35
Grant, Harvey, 33
Gross, Bob, 5, 8, 13

Hawes, Steve, 13
Hollins, Lionel, 5, 14, 17

Kersey, Jerome, 22, 25, 27–29
Khryapa, Viktor, 38

Lever, Fat, 21
Lucas, Maurice, 5–6, 8, 9, 13–14, 16–17, 19

Matthews, Wesley, 40
McMillan, Nate (coach), 38
Memorial Coliseum, 7, 21, 33
Miller, Andre, 40

Natt, Calvin, 17, 20–21
NBA Finals
   1977, 5–9, 13, 17, 28–29
   1990, 28–29
   1992, 28, 30–31

Oden, Greg, 40
Owens, Tom, 16–17

Paxson, Jim, 17, 19–20, 22–23
Petrie, Geoff (player and general manager), 11, 12, 13, 22
Pippen, Scottie, 35, 36
Porter, Terry, 23–24, 27–29, 30, 32–33
Pritchard, Kevin (coach), 37–38

Ramsay, Jack (coach), 6, 12–13, 14, 15, 20, 23–24, 28
Randolph, Zach, 36–37, 39

Rider, Isaiah, 35
Robinson, Cliff, 29, 32–33
Rose Garden, 7, 33
Roy, Brandon, 39–41

Sabonis, Arvydas, 32, 35
Schonely, Bill (announcer), 9
Schuler, Mike (coach), 24–25, 27, 28
Smith, Steve, 35
Steele, Larry, 6, 13
Stoudamire, Damon, 35
Strickland, Rod, 32–33

Thomas, Tyrus, 38
Thompson, Bernard, 22
Thompson, Mychal, 17, 19–20, 22–23
Todd, Rolland (coach), 11
Twardzik, Dave, 5, 13

Vandeweghe, Kiki, 22–24

Wallace, Rasheed, 33, 35–37
Walton, Bill, 5–6, 8–9, 12–17, 19
Wells, Bonzi, 35
Wicks, Sidney, 12
Wilkens, Lenny (coach), 12, 15

About the Author

Travis Clark is a freelance writer based in the Washington DC area. He is the author of five books for young adults.